An Interview
with
Abraham Lincoln

Also by Wade Hall

Reflections of the Civil War in Southern Humor (1962)

*The Smiling Phoenix:
Southern Humor, 1865–1914* (1965)

*The Truth Is Funny:
A Study of Jesse Stuart's Humor* (1970)

The High Limb: Poems by Wade Hall (1973)

This Place Kentucky (1975)

The Kentucky Book (1979)

*The Rest of the Dream:
The Black Odyssey of Lyman Johnson* (1988)

*Greetings from Kentucky:
A Post Card Tour, 1900-50* (1994)

*Sacred Violence:
A Reader's Companion to Cormac McCarthy* (1995)

A Visit with Harlan Hubbard (1995)

*Passing for Black: The Life and Careers
of Mae Street Kidd* (1996)

Complete Conviction: The Private Life of Wilson W. Wyatt (1996)

Hell-Bent for Music: The Life of Pee Wee King (1996)

*One Man's Lincoln: Billy Herndon (Honestly)
Represents Abe* (1997)

James Still: Portrait of the Artist as a Boy in Alabama (1998)

Waters of Life from Conecuh Ridge: The Clyde May Story (2003)

*Conecuh People: Words of Life from the
Alabama Black Belt* (2004)

An Interview with Abraham Lincoln

April 1, 1865

Wade Hall

NewSouth Books
Montgomery | Louisville

NewSouth Books
105 S. Court Street
Montgomery, AL 36104

Copyright © 2010 by Wade Hall. All rights reserved under International and Pan-American Copyright Conventions. Published in the United States by NewSouth Books, a division of NewSouth, Inc., Montgomery, Alabama.

Library of Congress Cataloging-in-Publication Data

Hall, Wade H.
An interview with Abraham Lincoln :
April 1, 1865 / Wade Hall.

p. cm.

ISBN-13: 978-1-58838-256-6
ISBN-10: 1-58838-256-7

1. Lincoln, Abraham, 1809-1865—Fiction. I. Title.
PS3558.A3756I58 2010
813'.54—dc22

2010011631

Design by Randall Williams

Printed in the United States of America
by Thomson-Shore, Inc.

An earlier version of this text,
ISBN 978-0-9662947-1-2, was published in 2008 by
the Kentucky Humanities Council, Inc.,
Lexington, Kentucky.

Contents

Author's Note / 7

The Interview / 11

A Lincoln Chronology / 73

Sources of Illustrations / 87

About the Author / 88

"The Last Offer of Reconciliation" is an 1865 lithograph dedicated to the memory of Lincoln and symbolizing the hopefulness of the nation at the end of the Civil War. Before a small temple where Liberty sits, Lincoln extends his hand to Jefferson Davis. Five of the temple columns bear the names of the states of the Union, while generals Sherman and Grant affix a ribbon with the names of the seceded states onto the sixth column.

Author's Note

This book is adapted from an earlier edition I prepared for the state humanities council in Kentucky, where I lived at the time, for distribution during the 2009 celebration of Lincoln's two hundredth birthday.

The content of the book—structured around an "interview" with the sixteenth president—is based on historical material, and the bulk of the words spoken by Lincoln are from the historical record. But no such interview actually took place, and the Shelby Grider who conducted the "interview" is a fictional character created for the purpose of this examination of Lincoln's views and philosophy.

Once I came up with the idea of using a fictional interviewer, I had to create a background story for him. I imagined him this way ...

... Shelby Grider was a native of Bowling Green, Kentucky. He and his younger brother, Christopher, were students at Georgetown College in Kentucky when the Confederates fired on Fort Sumter in 1861. The night after the attack on Sumter, Christopher, a sophomore, was with students who raised a Rebel flag to the top of Giddings Hall. The next day

Shelby and a band of Union boys stormed the hall to replace it with the American flag. Before they had finished their work, the Rebel students attacked.

Fists and blood were flying when the college president restored order. He lined up the Confederate boys on the south side of the college lawn and the Union boys on the north side. On his signal, the two sides about-faced and marched off to war. Christopher went his way, and Shelby his.

Shelby enlisted in a Union company in Louisville and was in skirmishes around Munfordville and Bowling Green. Then he went to Pittsburg Landing on the Tennessee River, where his Kentucky regiment joined General Ulysses S. Grant at Shiloh in the spring of 1862. Near the end of the battle, Shelby was wounded just below the left knee as the Rebels withdrew toward Corinth.

Shelby was separated from his company and bleeding so badly that he passed out. When he came to, a man in gray was bending over him, offering a drink of water from his canteen. The Rebel soldier unbuttoned his shirt and ripped it into strips, then took off Shelby's left boot, cut off the bottom of his trouser leg and bound up the wound.

When the bleeding stopped, Shelby asked meekly, "Why are you doing this? We are enemies." The Rebel smiled and answered, "I was in the Mexican War when Northern boys and Southern boys fought together. Don't you know that when the minié balls are flying and the artillery is hot as hell, there is no enemy but death? We are all brothers." Then he straightened up and walked away.

Soon Union medics found Shelby and took him to a field hospital, where a surgeon cleaned his wound and reset his broken bone. He eventually was moved to a military hospital in Louisville.

In Louisville he met George Prentice, editor of the Journal. *When Shelby was released from service, Prentice offered him a job writing for his paper.*

Shelby arrived in Washington, D.C., on March 31, 1865, still on crutches from his war wound. He stayed the night in the comfortable Willard Hotel. The next morning, refreshed, he made his way to the White House.

Shelby Grider walked into President Abraham Lincoln's White House office two days before the president left Washington for Richmond to reclaim Virginia and her Southern sisters for the Union. President Lincoln rose and extended his hand to the young man. The president motioned the guest to sit, then took Shelby's crutches and leaned them against his desk. He then sat facing the young reporter, ready for the interview . . .

President Abraham Lincoln, November 1863.

The Interview

President Abraham Lincoln: Welcome to the White House, Mr. Grider.

Shelby Grider: Mr. President, thank you for giving me a few minutes of your time. I know you are immensely busy with winding up the war and binding up the wounds it inflicted on our people and our country.

Lincoln: Were you wounded in the war?

Grider: Yes, sir, with Grant at Shiloh in '62.

Lincoln: And where are you from, son?

Grider: I'm from Bowling Green, Kentucky, but now I live in Louisville and work for the *Journal*.

Lincoln: Ah, Louisville, one of my favorite towns. It's been a vital supply and medical center for our troops coming down from Ohio and Indiana and the upper Midwest. I have many friends there. One of the first heroes of this war was Union major Robert Anderson, the Louisvillian in command of Fort Sumter. He refused to surrender the fort to the Confederates, and that's what started the war. The Rebels fired the first shot and soon occupied the fort. Thank God it's about over. Now, Shelby, I am happy to spend some time with you. I always have time to talk with a fellow Kentuckian.

Grider: Sir, do you still consider yourself a Kentuckian?

Lincoln: I certainly do. Indeed, I kept up with conditions in Kentucky by reading the *Louisville Journal* and the *Lexington Observer* and *Reporter*. Kentucky is where I was born and where I made my first memories. I lived in Kentucky until I was eight; then my family started moving west, first to Indiana and then to Illinois. That's a very Kentucky thing to do. After all, Daniel Boone wound up in Missouri. At least we didn't go that far. Whether I was living in Indiana or Illinois, I knew that Kentucky was only a few miles away. To this day, in fact, some of my best friends are Kentuckians, beginning with my wife. Just a joke, son. You'll get used to my backwoods sense of humor.

Grider: Yes, sir.

Lincoln: Relax, son. You are thrice welcome: as an American, as a Kentuckian, and as a scribe from the *Louisville Journal*. Your editor, George Prentice, didn't support me for president, but, when it was crucial, he supported the Union and urged Kentucky to stay with it. And so it did. Mr. Prentice is a Connecticut Yankee who came to Kentucky to write the campaign biography of my idol, Henry Clay, the Whig who deserved to become president but never did. My other idol, Thomas Jefferson, did succeed, and he became our greatest president.

Grider: I was a youngster when Mr. Clay died. What attracted you to him?

Lincoln: Mr. Clay, a great senator and orator, was totally devoted to the Union. At that time, my views on slavery were similar to his. Although he was a slave owner himself and opposed efforts to interfere with slavery where it already existed, he opposed extension of slavery into the new western states. He eventually realized, as I have, that any slavery in this country is a blot on American democracy. and he became an advocate of gradual emancipation.

Grider: I know he ran for president several times, but I was too young to vote for him.

Lincoln: Yes, he did. His first run was in 1824, when he ran fourth out of four candidates. He attacked the rabid abolitionists in 1839 and said he would "rather be right than president." Then he lost the Whig nomination in 1840 to William Henry Harrison, who was elected president. He won the Whig nomination in 1844 but lost the presidency to James K. Polk, a Democrat. His last chance was 1848, when he lost the Whig nomination to the hero of the Mexican War, Zachary Taylor, who, as you know, became president. It's tough to defeat a war hero in any election. But I supported Senator Clay every time he ran.

Grider: When did you get the itch to go into politics?

Lincoln: I'd been thinking about it for some time, but it was around '32 that I decided to run for the Illinois legislature. I was a greenhorn and not a very effective campaigner, and I lost. I did right well around my home, New Salem, where I got 277 out of 300 votes, but my support lagged a bit everywhere else. Two years later, fortified with the knowledge that you can only learn from defeat, I ran again and was elected. In December of 1834, I took my first elective office in Vandalia, which was then the capital of Illinois. A few years later, I helped get the capital moved closer to my law office in Springfield.

Grider: How did you choose your party?

Lincoln: When I was old enough to vote, I joined Henry Clay's party, the Whigs. The other party was the Democrats. The Republican Party was started later. A lot of our enemies called us Whigs the party of the rich, but

This is the earliest known photo of Lincoln, a daguerreotype made in 1846–47 when he was an Illinois congressman-elect.

I considered myself a political heir of Jefferson. I was a Jeffersonian and did not see the Democrats then as his rightful heirs. So I supported Clay in his campaigns and called the Democrats "Locofocos," a nickname we gave to some wild Democrats up in New York. Sometimes I'd be campaigning for Clay and somebody would say, "Well, Abe, how can you tell that them folks ain't Jeffersonian Democrats? How can you tell the difference between a real Democrat and a Locofoco?"

I said, "Well, let me explain it with a story. Down in my home state of Kentucky one night, an old farmer was roused from his bed by a big racket in his henhouse. He lit a candle, took his gun, and went down to the henhouse. Inside, he moved his light around in the darkness and spied the cause of all the ruckus. It was a polecat crouched in a corner, surrounded by two or three dead chickens. The polecat looked at the farmer and began defending himself in his own language, saying he was no killer, no thief, just an innocent animal, a friend of the farmer who'd come inside the henhouse to watch over the chickens. But that polecat wasn't as smart as he thought. He couldn't fool the farmer, who said, "Yeah? You look to me like a polecat. You're just the size of a polecat. You behave like a polecat." Then he pinched his nose together and said, "And you surely smell like a polecat. And, as God is my witness, you are a polecat! Innocent and good as you say you are, by God, I'll kill you!" And he did. Then he dragged the creature outside and examined him up close with his candle, and sure enough, he was a polecat.

"Now, friends and fellow citizens," I said, "these Locofocos in Illinois claim to be true Democrats, but they are only Locofocos. Just like that farmer with the polecat, they look like Locofocos, they're just the size of Locofocos, they behave like Locofocos." Then I pinched my nose with my fingers and concluded, "They smell like Locofocos; and by God, they are Locofocos." Everybody laughed, both Whigs and Democrats. Yes, sir, I learned when I was starting out that a funny story will win an election over policy almost every time. It's how I won my race for Congress in 1847 against the venerable Methodist circuit rider, Brother Peter Cartwright, the Democratic candidate. He might have been a better orator than I was, but I told better stories.

Grider: When you and Senator Stephen Douglas were debating each other in 1854 for the U.S. Senate, was he a better storyteller than you?

Lincoln: I don't know. But I do know he was a very good debater and a worthy opponent. Slavery was becoming the burning issue of the time. I was still forming my policy, and maybe I went a little too far in one of my speeches. Maybe the people of Illinois were not ready for what I said in my speech at the close of the Republican state convention that nominated me for the Senate. It was certain that the Illinois legislature was not ready because they chose Douglas over me.

Grider: Mr. Lincoln, what did you say?

Lincoln: I think I was too radical. I looked too far ahead. The nation was rapidly becoming divided by slavery. Compromises worked only partly and only for a while. Now we were facing another time of decision. We must choose what we will be, a slave nation or a free nation. We cannot continue to be both. In my concluding remarks I said, "A house divided against itself cannot stand. I believe this government cannot endure permanently half slave and half free. I do not expect the Union to be dissolved; I do not expect the house to fall; but I do expect it will cease to be divided. It will become all one thing, or all the other."

Grider: And that sentiment cost you the election to the Senate?

Lincoln: Yes, I'm sure it did. But I think it led to my election to the presidency. It was a crossroads the nation had reached, and a decision had to be made, sooner rather than later. Most people knew that to reimpose slavery on the entire nation was unthinkable. Yet it was not clear how

Lincoln statue in Freeport, Illinois, site of the second and most famous of the seven Lincoln-Douglas debates, August 27, 1958.

slavery would be abolished or what would happen to the freed slaves. What would it take to put the nation, once and for all, on the righteous road to the freedom that we had always claimed for ourselves, but not for everyone? Could it be done peacefully through the government, or would it take a war? Well, we found out.

When the Republican Party was formed in 1856, four years after Mr. Clay's death, I saw a chance to be an influence in a new party with a new agenda, a party dedicated to saving the Union and emancipating the slaves. General John C. Fremont was our first presidential candidate, but he lost to James Buchanan. I won in 1860, despite my lack of Kentucky's support, Kentucky was having its own internal struggle because it was pro-Union and also pro-slavery. I suppose Kentuckians thought this new party was simply too radical for them, so they gave their twelve electoral votes to John Bell of the Constitutional Union Party, which hoped to save the Union by proposing a compromise on slavery.

Senator John J. Crittenden said his home state of Kentucky was the very "heart of the Union" and would never secede. He was right, but there were times when I feared Kentucky would sever its ties with the Union and join the Confederacy. That would have been a disaster for both Kentucky and the Union.

Through the dark, bitter days of this war, I never lost

contact with Kentucky. I kept in close touch with special friends and supporters in Lexington and Louisville. I was especially concerned about Western Kentucky and the Bluegrass of Central Kentucky, where slavery was so important to the culture and the economy. The mountain counties had few slaves and were the most loyal.

I also appreciated the support of Cassius Marcellus Clay, but I worried initially that his radical position on abolition would agitate the moderates so much he would turn them toward secession. I appointed him minister to Russia soon after I took office, then brought him back to Kentucky on a special mission to test the waters for a proclamation of partial emancipation. After assessing the effects of the proclamation on the pro-slavery Unionists, Clay assured me they would remain loyal. About three weeks later, after our victory at Antietam and confident that Kentucky would stay in the Union, I issued the proclamation.

Grider: You certainly succeeded in pacifying Kentuckians into staying with the Union.

Lincoln: Yes, I worked hard at it from the beginning. After I had won the presidency in 1860, I stopped in Cincinnati on my way by train to Washington to be inaugurated. And I tried again to reason with the citizens of my beloved Kentucky. I said, "I hold no bitterness against my brother Kentuckians for voting so overwhelmingly against me. I understand." Later, when Governor Beriah Magoffin wrote to remind me that Kentucky was neutral and that he expected me to respect that neutrality, I wrote back, politely but firmly, "I most cordially sympathize with Your Excellency in the wish to preserve the peace of my native state, but it is with regret I search, and cannot find, in your not very short letter any declaration or intimation that you entertain any desire for the preservation of the Federal Union." He tried to sever Kentucky from the Union, but he didn't succeed.

If Kentucky had seceded with its mother state of Virginia, the war might have been fought north of the Ohio River with a very different outcome. Kentucky's location made it strategic for the preservation of the Union. Look at the map, beginning with Delaware and Maryland and the new state of West Virginia, and follow the Ohio River down to Missouri. Kentucky was like the keystone in a great arch that holds the other stones together. If Kentucky had fallen to the Confederacy, I feared the other border states between North and South would have left the Union. These United States would have crumbled and we would have become two nations, despite all that I could do.

I am mindful that out of some 150,000 votes cast in Kentucky during the 1860 election, I received fewer than 1,400. In all of Fayette County, I collected a grand total of five votes, only two of which came from Lexington, Mrs.

Lincoln's hometown. Even though I didn't win Kentucky's electoral votes in 1860, in the months before the election, I took advantage of every opportunity to appeal to Kentuckians to stay in the Union. In September of 1859, I spoke in Cincinnati and addressed specific remarks on slavery to "my fellow Kentuckians" across the river. I pleaded with Kentuckians to be reasonable because, I said, "There is room for all of us to be free." I still believe that.

Grider: When you ran for reelection, many people thought you might lose the presidency to General George McClellan. Still, you won.

Lincoln: Yes, I did, but McClellan wasn't much of a hero. When he was in charge of our armies, we almost lost the war.

We certainly didn't have the best generals, did we? I discovered early in the war that the South had the best generals. I even tried to get General Lee to command our forces. My generals sometimes drank too much and fought too little.

General McClellan wouldn't push the enemy hard enough. He'd win a small skirmish, then retreat, and lose the advantage. After one short encounter with the enemy, he wired me, "We have just captured six cows. What shall we do with them?" I quickly responded, "Milk them." You don't win battles and wars if you spend too much time capturing cows and you are too timid to fight the other side.

Now General Grant sometimes drank too much, but, when given the chance, he knew how to win battles. Except for serious mistakes at Shiloh, Grant fought brilliantly. One day a delegation of Grant critics came to me and demanded that I replace him. I said, "Why?" They said, "Why, Mr. President, he drinks." I said, "Well, now, does any one of you know which brand of whiskey he drinks? If it's whiskey that makes him behave as he does on the battlefield, I'll order a barrel of it sent to every general in our army."

You know, son, one of the evils of war is what it does to civilians. War should always be a last resort; and because of the terrible toll this war has taken on everybody, sometimes I'm not sure it's justified even then. Civil wars are the worst kind because they tear families and towns and states apart. It's the horror of brother killing brother.

Grider: Yes, sir, it is. My brother Christopher fought with General Bragg at Perryville and lost his life. Chris slipped away to get a drink of water at Doctor's Creek and was shot by a Union sniper. Several weeks later my father and I drove a wagon from Bowling Green to Perryville and dug up my brother and took his body back home for a decent burial. It was a hard thing to do.

Lincoln: My deepest sympathies to you and your family, son.

Grider: Thank you very much, sir. I have heard that you have some military experience. Can you tell me about it?

Lincoln: Well, let's put it this way: I'm probably a lot better at commander-in-chiefing than I was in commanding a small company. My war story is short and modest. In the spring of 1832, when I was about twenty-three, I was elected captain of a volunteer unit that fought in the Black Hawk War.

Not many people have heard of it. It wasn't much of a war—more like a series of short skirmishes. Neither side was much inclined to fight. I don't believe anybody was killed on either side. Not more than two hundred Indians, led by Chief Black Hawk, were coming east across the Mississippi River to find food. According to treaty they were not allowed to do this. But they were having a famine in their country and were hungry. So about a thousand of us soldiers spent three months chasing the chief and his men back across the river.

I wasn't much of an expert on military tactics or protocol and didn't inspire much confidence in my men. One day I was drilling my men across a field when they approached a gate leading into another field. To save my soul, I couldn't remember the command to have the men change marching formation so that they could pass through the narrow gate. As the men neared the gate, I shouted desperately, "This company is dismissed for two minutes; then we will fall in again on the other side of this damned fence!"

Once I accidentally shot off my rifle in camp and had my sword taken away for a day as punishment. Another time some of the boys in my company stole some liquor and got too drunk to march the next day. I was punished for not having them under control and had to carry a wooden sword for two days. Finally, we won our glorious victory and sent Black Hawk and his braves back to the western side of the river, and we were ready to go home to New Salem. I had to walk all the way because someone had stolen my horse. And that's the story of my inglorious career as a soldier.

Grider: Sir, you've been criticized by your generals for the number of pardons you've given to soldiers convicted of desertion and other military breaches.

Lincoln: Yes, I have. But I don't believe in Old Testament punishments like stoning and eye-for-an-eye justice. If somebody makes a mistake and has to be disciplined, I'd like to punish him humanely and err on the side of mercy. That's why I've pardoned dozens of soldiers who deserted on the battlefield. Deciding what is just has been one of the heaviest burdens of my presidency. I've had so many mothers and fathers pleading for their sons' lives, so many of my wife's relatives and friends asking for help.

I do get weary. Seldom has a day passed that I've not been petitioned and hounded by someone who wants a government job or a pardon. I am not gifted with the wisdom of Solomon. But I have tried to be generous to both sides. I want to reunite this broken nation, and meting out justice leavened with mercy is a start.

Grider: Sir, some Southerners and Yankee Copperheads have maintained that the main issue in this war has been states' rights. But wasn't it mainly about slavery?

Lincoln: Of course, it was about slavery. At first, I thought slavery was a secondary issue. But my position began to change. Eventually, for me, slavery came to be not just the central issue of the war but the central moral issue of our national history. So I couldn't please anybody, at either extreme or in the middle. On the one hand, the abolitionists attacked me for not acting sooner. Then when I issued my Emancipation Proclamation, people thought I'd gone either too far or not far enough. Young man, one of the first lessons a politician learns is that you can't please all the people all the time. You simply have to do what you think is right and hope that at least a majority of the people agree with you at election time.

Slavery was a volatile issue from the beginning. It split the country when I was elected and the Southern states began to secede. But I couldn't please some Northern people either. A New York abolitionist said to me one day, "Mr. President, what are you waiting for? You should have freed the slaves on your first day in office." I said, "My family never owned slaves in Kentucky, and even when I was a boy, I knew in my heart that slavery was wrong. After my family moved to Indiana then Illinois, I could see slaves working on the Ohio River boats, and I saw slaves in chains being sold and taken to work in the cotton and cane fields of the lower South. And when, as a young man, I went downriver all the way to New Orleans and saw the condition of slaves down there, I made up my mind that, if I ever had the chance, I would do something about it." My visitor replied, rightly so, "Well, it's time you did," and walked out of the room.

But in politics you have to proceed carefully. I had to be cautious about the slave issue, or I would have lost the support of many Northerners who opposed secession but not slavery. After all, slavery was woven into the fabric of American history. All the original thirteen states at one time had slaves. Unfortunately, the idea persists in the North that even free black people are not quite as human as white people. We also have to remember that many of the slaves were brought into this country on Yankee ships

1896 Emancipation Proclamation poster, by A. B. Daniel, Sr., printed in Tuscaloosa, Alabama, by the Enquirer Job Printing Co.

and that the Northern states abolished slavery principally because it was not profitable. So I had to wait until the time was right to announce the Emancipation Proclamation, and I had to tie it to the states in active rebellion against the Union. Yes, it was as much a political document as it was a moral document. It had to be. Sometimes, rightly or wrongly, even presidents have to compromise.

If I hadn't, it might have been like the barber in Illinois shaving a fellow who had a hatchet face and lantern jaws like mine. The barber stuck his finger in his customer's mouth to make his cheek stick out. Unfortunately, while he was shaving the man, he went too far and cut through the fellow's cheek and cut off his own finger. I didn't want to cut off my finger if I didn't need to.

Grider: What a good way to explain your dilemma.

Lincoln: Well, as a boy and a young man, I learned from teachers, preachers, and a few good politicians how to get your point across without preaching. A good story can sometimes get your point across without insulting or angering people.

One of the first problems I had to tackle was how to pacify politicians who had their own agenda. One day a state governor came to the White House fuming about the draft quota for his state. He had visited Secretary of War Stanton but couldn't get any satisfaction. Finally, he burst into my office, and I managed to tame him with a story about an old farmer in Illinois who had a huge stump in his field. It was an eyesore and an obstacle. One day he showed up at the general store and announced that he'd solved the problem of the stump. The boys hanging out in the store asked him how he did it, by cutting it up or pulling it out with a team of horses. Finally, he whispered his solution: "I just plowed around it." That's the way I did with the governor. It took me three hours but I finally plowed around him with stories and other distractions. He left my office not knowing he had been bamboozled.

But to get back to the slavery issue. When I wrote my first inaugural address, I knew in my heart that slavery was the problem that was tearing our country apart, and I said: "One section of the country believes slavery is right, and ought to be extended, while another believes it is wrong, and ought not to be extended. This is the only substantial dispute." What I was really saying is this: If slavery is wrong today, it has always been wrong; and it's time we rooted it out.

Grider: Mr. President, your use of humor has been criticized during this time of war.

Lincoln: I like funny stories and I like to read the humor of Artemus Ward and Petroleum Nasby. Sometimes late at night, I run around the White House looking for an

Lincoln told a good yarn, and enjoyed one.

audience to entertain with their latest stories.

One day Senator Ben Wade came to my office to criticize my handling of the war. While he was raving at me, I said, "You remind me of a story I heard back in Kentucky." Whereupon Wade jumped up and shouted, "The story be damned! The country is falling apart and you sit here telling stories. You would tell stories if you were only a mile from Hell!" I said, "Well, Senator, it's just about a mile from here to the Capitol." He didn't laugh, but I think he got my message.

I learned a lot from my experiences growing up and from the stories I heard. Not only did they help me solve problems, but the laughter has also helped relieve the tension of the burden I have been carrying as president.

I think I would have gone crazy if I hadn't had the safety valve of humor. One day I was being driven along a bumpy road to the scene of a recent battle near Washington. Suddenly, the driver stopped the carriage to do a minor repair and started cussing. When he finished, I tapped him on the shoulder and said, "Beg your pardon, son, what church do you go to?" The driver said, "I'm a Methodist." I said, "Well, that's mighty strange. You cuss just like the secretary of state, Mr. Seward, and he's an Episcopalian!" We had a good laugh and felt better.

It's true that my sense of humor helped me survive not only the war but also the radical Republicans who kept hounding me to do it their way, everything from battle strategy to the immediate emancipation of the slaves.

Three men in Congress—Senators Charles Sumner and Henry Wilson of Massachusetts and Congressman Thad Stevens of Pennsylvania—kept pestering me to issue an emancipation proclamation, and I kept saying I'd do it when the time was right. One day I was conferring with another set of self-styled policy experts, and I had just about lost my patience and my manners. I looked out my office window and saw the Radical Three walking rapidly across the lawn in my direction.

I turned to my guests and said, "I'm reminded of when I was a schoolboy, and we would line up and take turns reading aloud from the Bible. One time a little fellow was given the verse in the Old Testament Book of Daniel that has in it the names of Shadrach, Meshach, and Abednego, the three men who were cast by Babylonian king Nebuchadnezzar into the fiery furnace. But they were delivered by an angel. Of course, the boy couldn't pronounce those names, so the schoolmaster rapped him across the knuckles and sent him to the end of the line. The reading continued until it got to be the little man's turn to read again, and he began to howl like a coyote. 'Boy, what's wrong with you?' the master asked. The boy pointed to the new verse he was supposed to read and wailed, 'Lookee thar! Here comes them damn three fellers again!'" Then I called my visitors to the window and said, "Now lookee thar at my damn three fellers." And there were Sumner, Wilson, and Stevens about to enter the White House and heading for my office. They got the point, too.

Grider: Mr. President, will you talk a little about your family and your boyhood?

Lincoln: Sure I will. In 1816, when I was seven, my family left Hardin County, Kentucky, but I have some good memories of my native state. Of course, I may have picked up some of my memories from my family, but we all do that. And even after we moved to Indiana and Illinois, I made frequent trips back to Kentucky.

My father told me what little he knew of the Lincoln family history. It seems that wherever we lived in the old countries of Europe or in the new land of America, we were common, undistinguished people. We were not the first explorers or settlers of Kentucky, but the family arrived well before Kentucky was admitted to the Union and while the land was still mostly a wilderness. My English ancestors had come to America in the seventeenth century and settled first in Pennsylvania; then in 1750 they moved to the Shenandoah Valley of Virginia. And in 1780 my grandfather Abraham Lincoln, after whom I am named, came to settle several hundred acres of land on the Green River in what was then Lincoln County. They later moved to Washington County, where my mother, Nancy Hanks, and father, Thomas, married in 1806. I know very little about my mother or her family.

Like a lot of Kentuckians in those days, we were a restless family, so my parents moved to Hardin County and lived in Elizabethtown, where my sister Sarah was born. I was born on February 12, 1809, near Hodgenville at the Sinking Spring Farm, for which my father, Thomas, had paid $200 for three hundred acres. We lived in a one-room log cabin with no floor except the earth. From there we moved to yet another farm nearby that we called the Knob Creek Farm. My first distinct memories are from this location. My brother, Thomas Jr., was born there, and it's where he died when he was still a baby. For two terms Sarah and I went to the local school; then we all piled into an oxcart and left Kentucky permanently.

From Hodgenville we went through Elizabethtown and Vine Grove to Cloverport, where we crossed the Ohio River and settled on new land in southern Indiana. This was the 160 acres that my father had already staked out in the wilderness about seventeen miles north of the Ohio River. This was in the fall of 1816. We built a crude hut before winter set in. During the spring we cleared enough land for a crop of corn and a vegetable garden. I was getting some size on me and beginning to learn how to use an ax to good advantage. I even split a few rails for

The cabin where Lincoln was born in 1809, as preserved within the Lincoln Memorial at Hodgenville, Kentucky.

a fence to keep the larger wild animals from eating our corn. Here I spent a few more months in school.

Grider: Did you have any contact with relatives back in Kentucky?

Lincoln: Not much. Occasionally a new settler would come in from Kentucky and live nearby. In 1827, eleven years after we had moved to Indiana, I got into trouble with the Commonwealth of Kentucky when the Kentucky authorities caught me operating a ferry across the Ohio without a license. I pleaded my own case before a magistrate in his house near Hawesville, Kentucky, and won! I reckon from then on I was destined—or doomed—to become a lawyer.

Grider: You lost your mother when you were still young.

Lincoln: Yes, and I was devastated by her death. It wasn't long after we had left Kentucky. She died in October 1818 of the milk sickness. Apparently, the illness was caused by a poisonous plant called snakeroot. When cows sometimes ate it, it would contaminate their milk. She was buried not far from our cabin. A year later a Baptist preacher from Hardin County came and preached her funeral. I loved my mother very much and don't believe for a moment the rumors that Thomas Lincoln was not my blood father and that a man named Abraham Enloe, who also lived in Hardin County, was actually my father. I don't think there is any evidence to prove that rumor or any of the others that have circulated around me since I became a politician.

Grider: Then your father remarried?

Lincoln: Yes. He went back to Kentucky, to Elizabethtown, and married Sarah Bush Johnston, a widow with three children. Her family was fairly well-off and was better educated than the Lincolns. My father had courted her before he married my mother, but she had refused him, so he said. This time, however, she accepted and moved with her children to our place in Indiana. It made a full house. By the time she arrived, the house was filthy and almost in shambles. She quickly made some needed changes. My stepmother had brought with her not only her passion for cleanliness and order but also such necessary household items as bedsteads, bedding, tables, chairs, cooking utensils, whale-oil lamps, a spinning wheel, and a loom. She soon persuaded my father to put a floor in the cabin and to install proper doors and windows. She tried to bring civilization to our rather wild backwoods family. She could read, and I think I got my own love of learning from her.

But I loved my own mother, too. Many years later, in the

fall of 1844, when I was electioneering for Henry Clay in southern Indiana, I stopped by the old home place, then in a state of disrepair. I visited the graveyard nearby where my mother and sister Sarah, who died when I was still a boy, were buried. It was a very emotional experience and called forth a piece of verse that, I hope, makes up in sincerity what it lacks in style and skill. May I read it to you?

Grider: Yes sir, please do.

Lincoln: It is called "My Childhood Home."

My childhood home again I see,
And gladden with the view;
And still as mem'ries crowd my brain,
There's sadness in it too.

O memory! Thou mid-way world
'Twixt Earth and Paradise;
Where things decayed, and loved ones lost
In dreamy shadows rise.

And freed from all that's gross or vile,
Seem hallowed, pure and bright,
Like scenes in some enchanted isle,
All bathed in liquid light.

Now twenty years have passed away,
Since here I bid farewell

To wood, and fields, and scenes of play
And schoolmates loved so well.

I range the fields with pensive tread,
I pace the hollow rooms;
And feel (companion of the dead)
I'm living in the tombs.

And now away to seek some scene
Less painful than the last,
With less of horror mingled in
The present and the past.

The very spot where grew the bread
That formed my bones, I see
How strange, old field, on thee to tread,
And feel I'm part of thee.

Well, it goes on for several more stanzas, but I think I've read you enough to show that I'm probably a better president than poet.

The next time our family moved was to a farm near Charleston, in eastern Illinois. I wasn't there long. I'd been doing some odd jobs up and down the Sangamon River, and a couple of times I helped take a flatboat of goods down to New Orleans on the Mississippi River.

When I was about twenty-two, I struck out on my own permanently and moved to New Salem, which had about thirty-five families and was the largest settlement I'd ever lived in. I began to develop some rather large ambitions, but first I had to improve myself. I found a local teacher who helped me with grammar and reading, and soon I was reading Benjamin Franklin's autobiography, the works of Voltaire, and Thomas Paine's *Age of Reason*, which helped me develop my own liberal religious views. I don't talk about religion very much with Mrs. Lincoln, but I dutifully attend an occasional service with her and the boys in the Presbyterian Church. It doesn't take a lot of time and it makes Mrs. Lincoln happy.

I enjoyed the rough-and-tumble life of the frontier in New Salem while I was trying to improve myself socially and economically. I went into the store business with William Berry, but we weren't very good at it. I was too fond of books and he was too fond of liquor. Berry died and left us with a debt of almost $1,200, which I finally managed to pay off. I joined the New Salem Debating Society, where I learned a lot that would help me when I went into lawyering. I also found out I could learn something useful from unlikely sources, even the town drunk, old Jack Kelso. One time I found him in a fight with another fellow, and Jack was getting beaten up, so I broke it up. Somebody said, "Abe, why did you take the part of that no-good bum?" I said, "I don't care what you folks do with the drunk part of him, but I will not allow you to thrash up the intelligent part of him because he's teaching me how to read Shakespeare, and I'm not yet through with my studies."

At New Salem I picked up other jobs. One time I was postmaster, and another time I was county land surveyor. As I became a better reader, I decided to read tougher books and borrowed some law books, which fascinated me. Before I knew it, I decided I'd move to town, to Springfield, and seek my fortune there and study the law; and that's where I lived until I came here to Washington to take this job.

Grider: What was Springfield like then?

Lincoln: It had a lot of Kentuckians in it. Most of them were several social classes above me, but I was learning to move in different circles—from the lowest to the highest, from the Jack Kelsos to the Speeds and Todds.

Grider: How did you meet Mr. Joshua Speed?

Lincoln: It was April 15, 1837. I rode into town from New Salem on a rented horse. I had all my belongings in my saddlebags. I stopped at Speed's store and went in to price some goods that I needed to set up housekeeping. The total came to $17. But I didn't have that kind of money, and Speed knew it. He suggested I could bunk with him upstairs over the store. I said it sounded like a good deal

1900 photo of the Lincolns' home in Springfield, Illinois.

to me and if he could allow my long legs to extend over the end of the bed we were to share, we'd make a go at it. It was the best contract I ever made. I went upstairs, dropped my saddlebags, and came down and said, "Speed, I've moved in." With the exception of my later marriage to Mary Todd, it was the most productive relationship I've ever had. I was twenty-eight. Speed was twenty-three. I had never had a close friend until I knew Joshua Speed.

Grider: What kind of friend were you looking for?

Lincoln: Someone who was different from my father. He and I had little in common. He was content to live the life to which he was born. I was not. I wanted to rise in the world. I wanted to know men who could teach me how to read and write better, and what to read and write. I never went to school more than a total of one year, but I had learned enough for a start from men who were themselves barely literate. Then I was on my own. Over the years, I managed to give myself an advanced education so I could hold my head up in the company of men who had college degrees. My favorite authors were Shakespeare and Robert Burns and the writers of history. I talked with men who had read the great books of our civilization. In their company, I pulled myself up. I wanted to move from being a physical laborer like my father to being an intellectual laborer. I wanted to do good things for myself, but I also wanted to do things that were good for other people.

I wanted to know men from whom I could learn, men who could challenge me, men who could encourage me, men who would stick by me during the dark times—someone like the man who became my closest friend, Joshua Speed. He was the first and only man or woman I could talk to intimately and honestly and rationally on any subject—philosophical, personal, or political. Of course, we liked and respected each other. Maybe that bond came from our being fellow Kentuckians and bedfellows for some four years when he was running a store in Springfield and I was just beginning to become a lawyer and politician.

Speed and I were so very different and, at times, so very alike. Most important, we learned to trust each other completely. He was from a wealthy, aristocratic family in Louisville, and he was better looking than I was. And we were both ambitious but in different ways. He was ambitious for a comfortable, cultured life like the family he had been born into. I wanted that, too, and a bit more than that. For four years we cultivated and challenged each other, debating politics, reciting poetry—his favorite poet was Lord Byron—and dreaming our futures. We both liked humor—sometimes of the raucous variety—and storytelling.

Part of the time we had two other roommates: Billy Herndon, who later became my law partner, and a fellow named Charles Hurst. Both of them were clerking in Speed's store. Speed and I were also politically in tune. We were both Whigs and supported Henry Clay and his ambition to become president. Speed was a ladies' man. I was not. He knew how to talk to women. I didn't.

Later, when the time came for us both to get married, we supported each other. His father died in early 1840, and his family needed him back home in Kentucky. By the summer of 1841, I was engaged but depressed about my scheduled marriage to Miss Todd, so I absented myself from the wedding. Instead, I skedaddled down to Kentucky to visit Speed at his family's estate at Farmington, and we consoled and counseled each other. He was also facing marriage. We concluded it was time for him to get married in Louisville and for me to get married in Springfield. He encouraged me to marry Mary Todd, and I encouraged him to marry Fanny Henning, whom he was courting. After he married, I checked with him, and he said it was better than he expected and recommended that I do the same. So on November 4, 1842, Mary Todd and I were married. I think both our marriages have been about as successful as most marriages are. I had four sons whom I adored. Unfortunately, he and his wife had no children.

Despite our differences on such matters as emancipation of slaves, Speed and I are still friends, and he has supported most of my policies. Absence doesn't make friendships stronger, however, and we have drifted some distance apart as friends. Yet he is still the one person in my whole life that I have felt closest to. While we were living together as friends, we opened up our hearts completely to one another. After I was elected president, I wanted him to come to Washington with me, but he declined. I've never had another friend like him.

Grider: Well sir, you've been lucky.

Lincoln: Yes, indeed. And there have been other good friends in Springfield and Washington. As a young lawyer, I was a junior partner first to John Todd Stuart and then to Stephen T. Logan. From both of these men, I learned how to be a lawyer. In the fall of 1844, I formed a new partnership with William H. Herndon, whom I knew when he was a clerk in Speed's store. Billy, who was about ten years my junior, became a close friend and a steadfast supporter. He was also a Kentuckian, from Greensburg, and to some extent he took the place of Speed, though we were never as intimate. We had a very successful law practice, one which I intend to resume once I complete my service here in Washington. We spent many hours discussing and debating politics. Both of us were Whigs and opposed slavery, but he was for immediate emancipa-

Lincoln's friend and law partner, William Herndon.

tion, and I had not yet reached that radical position. I was for saving the Union above all else.

I considered inviting Billy to serve with me in Washington, but I was afraid his excessive drinking would be a liability. He once headed the Temperance League in Springfield, but he had difficulty practicing what he was preaching. Nevertheless, he is a loyal friend and supporter, especially since I issued my Emancipation Proclamation, which legally freed all slaves in states or parts of states that were in rebellion against the Union. He said, of course, that I should have gone all the way and freed all the slaves everywhere in this country. But I told him that as president I sometimes have to make decisions that are not only morally right but also politically shrewd. I had to keep the support of some men, both North and South, who supported the Union but believed that slavery should not be tampered with where it already existed. I told Billy when I left for Washington I wanted to make him proud of me. I also said, "Keep up our office sign, Lincoln and Herndon. I'll be back."

I should mention several other men who are my good friends. Another fellow Kentuckian who migrated to Illinois was Orville Hickman Browning, whose father was a successful merchant and planter. He has served as a senator from Illinois and has been my trusted confidant and adviser. We were also both devout Whigs and made the transition to the new and progressive Republican Party when it was founded. Sadly, he wanted me to appoint him to the Supreme Court, but I had to pass over him three times because I feared he was temperamentally unsuited for that august position.

I cannot name certain other men as real friends, but I can call them men who were essential to my presidency and to our ultimate success in this war and who promise to be valuable in the peace and reconstruction that will follow. I will name only a few, but the list from which I select their names is a long one. I will begin with my secretary of state, William H. Seward of New York State, an independent-minded patriot and Unionist who reluctantly accepted his cabinet position in my administration, though he was skeptical of my ability to govern; but he has since become a loyal and indispensable member of my cabinet. I have been slow to get the best generals in position to win this war, but, when given the opportunity, Generals Grant, Sherman, and others have risen to the demands of war and have brought the struggle to a successful conclusion. I owe them an unpayable debt of gratitude.

Now, I must give praise and credit to my hardworking, ever-faithful private secretaries, John George Nicolay and John Hay. Their trust and loyalty and their youth have sustained me. Their rhetorical skills have improved many of my letters and public speeches and have made me sound more eloquent and expressive than I really am. Finally, I should mention a young man who has recently become very special to me. He is David Derickson, a Pennsylvania solider who is my permanent guard when I retreat to the Soldiers' Home for rest and recuperation. Without such friends as these, I could never have become a successful lawyer or politician, and I could never have survived these five years that I have served as president. I hope they will be with me to the end.

Grider: Mr. Lincoln, we've touched a bit on this already, but can you explain the kind of relationship that you had with your father?

Lincoln: I wasn't close to my father at all. He was always too busy to spend much time with me. We were different in temperament and interests. He was a farmer and carpenter, and I don't think he quite knew what to make of me and my interest in books. I think he was naturally suspicious of men who make their living with their heads and not their hands. But we got along with each other. On the other hand, I admired both my mother and my stepmother. They were positive influences on me. But other than my two mothers, I haven't known any woman to whom I've been very close.

Grider: Not even Miss Todd?

Daguerreotype of Mary Todd Lincoln, a companion to the one of her husband on page 15.

Lincoln: Well, we have been fairly close since she became Mrs. Lincoln—close enough to have had four boys.

Grider: Did you court other women before you married Miss Todd?

Lincoln: I'm not sure you could call it courting, but I got to know a number of women who could have become Mrs. Lincoln, beginning with Ann Rutledge, a young lady out at New Salem. Sadly, she died before we could determine whether either of us was serious about the other. I like the young ladies, of course, but to this day I don't feel comfortable around them. Before I moved to Springfield, I wasn't old enough or mature enough to even think about getting married. I hadn't met a lady who fit me. Then, after I moved to town, I was busy preparing myself for a career as a lawyer. After a while my circle of friends became large enough to include eligible women who were looking for husbands. This was when I kind of halfway courted Mary Owens, a Kentucky lady, but we broke it off mutually before it had gotten anywhere.

I generally am attracted to older women and feel closer to them than to their daughters. I like Mrs. Lucy Speed very much. She is Joshua's mother and mistress of Farmington, their beautiful farm near Louisville. When I visited Joshua's home right after my temporary breakup

President and Mrs. Lincoln, with sons Robert Todd and Thomas (Tad); of the Lincolns' four sons, only Robert lived to adulthood.

with Mary Todd, I was depressed and melancholy, but Mrs. Speed cheered me up and made me feel like one of the family. She even assigned a servant to look after me while I was there. Of course, I liked all of Joshua's family. His brothers and sisters were hospitable and kind to me. A few months ago I appointed Joshua's brother James to be U.S. attorney general. It was a wonderful family. It was the kind of family I wish I could have had when I was growing up. It was the kind of family I wanted to have with Mary Todd.

Grider: Tell me about the breakup with Miss Todd.

Lincoln: I met her when she came to Springfield from her home in Lexington, and I liked her even though we were from different worlds. Like the Speeds in Louisville, her family were Kentucky gentry, with fine homes and servants and courtly manners. They were people who gave orders. My family was from the bottom of society. They were poor, working people who took orders. They worked like slaves to cut paths through the wilderness, clear the fields and plant and harvest the crops, and barely survived. If my family had remained in Kentucky and I had become a farmer or carpenter like my father, none of the Speeds or the Todds would have even spoken to me if we had passed in the road.

But we lived in a more egalitarian society in Illinois,

and also I had tried to improve myself so that I could feel comfortable with such people as the Todds and the Speeds. So I met Miss Todd. We became engaged and even set a date for our marriage. Like a lot of young bridegrooms, I got cold feet and skedaddled down to Louisville to visit my dear friend Joshua and to think about my future. For two weeks we shared our fears and our plans for our lives. He already knew that his life would be lived in Kentucky. I knew that whatever life I had before me would be grounded in Illinois. We both needed wives for our futures. So I went back to Springfield, mended my relationship with Miss Todd, and we were married.

Grider: What changed your mind about Miss Todd?

Lincoln: I decided I loved her. In my way, I did. I may not have been as affectionate as she wanted, but we learned to live together and be as close as most husbands and wives are. If I was going to be a successful politician, I had to have a wife, and she needed a husband. In fact, when she came out to Springfield from Lexington to visit her sister, she also came to look for a husband. The rumor went around that she said she was seeking a husband who would become president. In fact, she was courted for a while by Senator Stephen Douglas, whose presidential prospects then were certainly better than mine. I reckon she knew what she was doing when she chose me.

Grider: Yes, sir, I think she did. Has your family life been untroubled?

Lincoln: There are always family problems. No couples are completely compatible. Mary is high-strung and emotional, and I tend to be slower and more easygoing and sometimes get very depressed. But we have learned to tolerate each other's eccentricities. You know there have been stories that Mrs. Lincoln is a spy for the Confederacy and that she spends extravagant sums on her wardrobe. Well, she is no more a spy than I am. I don't know any information that she could have sent to General Lee or General Jackson about troop movements or battle strategy. As commander in chief, even I didn't have much knowledge that could have benefited the other side. She had brothers who fought for the Confederacy, and she loved them and wanted them safe. So did I. I wanted them to come back to the Union safely. Now, as to her extravagance, that's another story. Son, are you married?

Grider: No, sir.

Lincoln: Well, you probably don't understand women yet. I presume you had a mother, but a mother is different from a wife. Mothers worry about their children going naked and ragged. They want to keep them in clothes that are clean and mended. But wives love fashion and style and clothes for themselves that are up-to-date in Paris. Not Paris, Kentucky—Paris, France.

Mary was both a mother and a wife. She did a good job of keeping our boys in clean and decent clothes. She also did a good job of keeping herself in the latest fashions from Paris. Maybe I can explain that with a story. One evening, shortly after she had returned from a fashion trip to New York, Mrs. Lincoln swished into a White House reception trailing a long piece of fur behind her like a cat. She called it a "train." I said to a friend, "I see that our cat has a long tail tonight." He laughed. I walked over, and as I got closer, I saw how low-cut the neck of her dress was and whispered to Mary, "Mother, in my opinion, you'd be in better style if some of that tail were nearer the head!" She didn't laugh. After all, she wasn't the one born in a log cabin. She looked at me with icy eyes, threw back her head, and walked off.

Mary and I have had most of our arguments over money. She thought I gave away too much, and I thought she spent too much. She usually finds a way to get what she wants, and so do I. One day a young man came to my law office and solicited me for a donation to the Springfield Fire Brigade. I said, "I tell you what I'll do. Mrs. Lincoln is usually in good spirits after supper, so after eating this evening, I'll say, 'Well, Mother, I've been thinking of giving $50 to the fire brigade.' And she will say, 'Abe, you throw away too much money. Twenty dollars is quite enough.' So come by my house tomorrow and get your $20."

Grider: Mr. President, did you have a master plan that finally led you from a log cabin to the White House?

Lincoln: No, I don't think so. I admired President Jackson for having pulled himself up from his humble origins to the presidency, but I never dared to think it could happen to me. Not in the beginning. But I did have ambition.

I wanted to become a man of learning with a profession. I wanted to be literate and read books. I wanted to be a lawyer and win cases. I wanted to be a politician and win elections. As it turned out, my desire to rise above the poverty and ignorance of my birth took me down the road to this house, to this office, to this moment. Certainly, I could never have dreamed as a barefoot boy in Kentucky that one day I would be president. But as I look back over my life, it was a logical progression, step by step. And despite some missteps along the way, especially after I became president, I am satisfied with it—whether it was achieved by design and hard work, by luck, by Divine Providence or by a combination of those things.

Grider: Sir, can you say what is your proudest achievement as president?

Lincoln as presidential candidate, 1860.

Lincoln: Son, it's been an honor for a plain man like me to hold this high office. I never dreamed as a young rag-tailed boy in Kentucky, born in a small cabin with the earth as a floor, that I would someday become president of this glorious Union. I hope I've been an adequate husband to Mary and a good father to my sons, but as an American I'm proudest to have brought this nation back together, and I want to leave office soon with the Union not just intact but stronger than it's ever been. You know, your muscles get stronger when you pull on 'em and stretch 'em. I believe we've stretched this Union almost to the breaking point, and now that we're back together, we know we're indissoluble forever.

When I was riding out to the Soldiers' Home just a few days ago, a young fellow came hobbling up to me on a freshly carved hickory cane, still wearing his gray uniform—what was left of it—and he held out his hand and said, "Mr. Lincoln, I'm a Kentuckian from Bardstown, and I'm on my way home. Four years ago, we didn't know that we didn't have the right to secede; well, now we know. And the next time anybody tries to break up our Union, I'm gonna be the first man to enlist in your army." I got up and gave him a good Kentucky hug and said, "Welcome back, friend. We've missed you."

Grider: Mr. President, you're only fifty-six years old,

and you have many years ahead of you; but you've had a remarkable life already. Do you have any wisdom to give our readers in Kentucky?

Lincoln: Yes, I have learned two important lessons, one political and one personal. In my life they have been intertwined. First, this nation, this United States, imperfect though it is, is worth saving and improving, now and forever. Now the personal part. Where else could a poor boy like me rise to become head of his country? This honor and this burden, however, did not come easily. Real success comes to people who don't give up. I have failed so many times in so many ventures. I was a failure in business. I was a failure in love. And I was a failure in politics. Time and time again, I was rejected by the voters in Illinois when I ran for the legislature, for Congress, for the Senate. But I didn't let my failures discourage me. I kept on trying, and five years ago, I finally succeeded.

Grider: Sir, now that the war is almost over, what will you do with Mr. Davis and General Lee? Put them in prison? Or hang them?

Lincoln: Neither. I don't want revenge. I don't want anyone hurt in any way. I know a lot of Northerners want to lynch both Lee and Davis, but they are honorable men. Mr. Davis, like me, is a Kentuckian. While he was moving south to Mississippi, I was moving with my family north to Indiana and then to Illinois. We both became heavily influenced by where we lived.

General Lee is a gentleman and one of the greatest soldiers this nation has ever produced. When the war came on, we offered him command of all the Union forces, but he declined in favor of his native state of Virginia. I don't agree with his decision, but I understand it. He is still an honorable man. I welcome him back to the Union. He's still very popular in the South, of course, but in the Northern states as well. I believe he could run for president of these re-United States in a few years and win. I want all the Confederates to come home. Now we must bind up the wounds of the nation. We've hated each other long enough. We've shed too much blood on both sides.

Here's a story that will show you how I feel about what should happen as we bring this nation back together. I remember a boy back in Springfield who worked and saved his money to buy himself a pet raccoon. For a while, the boy enjoyed training and playing with his new friend, but soon the novelty wore off, and the boy found himself trapped with a frisky pet who tore his clothes and bit him. One day the boy was seen leading his raccoon through the streets on the end of a rotten rope. "This 'coon is so much trouble to me," he told a passerby, who then said, "Well, why don't you get rid of him?" The boy whispered,

"Hush. Don't tell anybody, but I'm letting him gnaw his way through this rope so I can tell folks he got away." That's what I'd like to do with Davis and Lee and all the high Confederates. I'd like for them to go their own way, be good citizens, and never bother me again.

But here's another story that may be more pertinent. General Sherman asked me the other day if I wanted him to capture Jeff Davis or let him escape. "Well, General," I said, "back in old Sangamon County, I used to know an old Irishman who was much too fond of drink. Every night he'd fill up with booze and wind up in the gutter face down. At last a local preacher got hold of the drunkard and made him join the temperance society. But it was only a few days before the old fellow had found his way back to the saloon. 'I'll have a lemonade,' he said to the shocked bartender, then added, 'but you can slip in a drop or two of gin if you do so unbeknownstlike.' And that's the way I feel about Jeff Davis. As president, I have to officially try to catch him; but it might be better for us all in the long run if you let him get away 'unbeknownstlike.'"

Grider: Mr. President, do you read the Bible?

Lincoln: Yes, I do, when I can find the time. It's one of the great books of our civilization. I favor the Gospels and the words of Jesus. He had it right. But sometimes I use the Old Testament when it's appropriate. I wasn't keen on running for a second term as president, but I decided I should. After all, I had helped get the country in a big mess, and I figured I should help to clean it up. But when I announced I would run a second time, I was warned that I was so unpopular that I wouldn't even get the Republican nomination, much less get reelected. I got depressed thinking about my reelection prospects. But I felt better when my main competitor, John Fremont, held a convention in Cleveland and drew only about four hundred people. I went around for several days reading with great enthusiasm 1 Samuel 22:2: "And everyone that was in distress, and everyone that was in debt, and everyone that was discontented gathered themselves unto him, and he became captain over them, and there were with him about 400 persons." I figured that it was a sign that I would be reelected.

Grider: Mr. President, now that it's almost over, do you think the war was worth the terrible cost in human lives and resources?

Lincoln: Yes, I have to believe it was. I shudder to think of what it has cost us. A whole generation of young men are killed and maimed. But I believe it was a necessary war. I don't believe we could have saved the country any other way. I pray that in the future we will find more humane ways of solving our disagreements. There have to be better

In his second inaugural address, March 1865, Lincoln famously declared, "With malice toward none, with charity for all, with firmness in the right as God gives us to see the right, let us strive on to finish the work we are in, to bind up the nation's wounds . . ., to do all which may achieve and cherish a just and lasting peace among ourselves and with all nations."

ways . . . there have to be. I hope no other president will be burdened as I have been. I hope no other president will have to write such a letter as this that I wrote last fall to a mother who had sacrificed all five of her sons. [He pulls the following letter from a drawer in his desk.]

> Executive Mansion
> Washington, Nov 21, 1864
>
> To Mrs Bixby, Boston, Mass,
>
> Dear Madam,
>
> I have been shown in the files of the War Department a statement of the Adjutant General of Massachusetts that you are the mother of five sons who have died gloriously on the field of battle. I feel how weak and fruitless must be any word of mine which should attempt to beguile you from the grief of a loss so overwhelming. But I cannot refrain from tendering you the consolation that may be found in the thanks of the republic they died to save. I pray that our Heavenly Father may assuage the anguish of your bereavement, and leave you only the cherished memory of the loved and lost, and the solemn pride that must be yours to have laid so costly a sacrifice upon the altar of freedom.
>
> Yours very sincerely and respectfully,
> A. Lincoln.

Grider: It's a beautiful letter. It must have been a great consolation to her.

Lincoln: I hope so. And I hope the country they helped re-create will be worthy of their lives.

Grider: Mr. President, what are your hopes for the future?

Lincoln: I hope I will be able to complete my presidency by reuniting our separated people into one people and into a union stronger than before. I hope we will repair the damages done to the people and the land by this war and make it again the healthy land of liberty and opportunity for all.

I hope we will welcome the freedmen and women into the fellowship of our one human family and educate and support them as they assume more and more rights and privileges of full citizenship in our one nation of free people. I hope we will move steadily and determinedly toward equality of opportunity for all our citizens. And I hope that brother will never again be called upon to fight his brother. I hope we never have to fight another war, but if we do, that it will be against an outside enemy who will not be reasoned with and who would do us harm.

Grider: And do you have regrets about your life or your presidency?

Lincoln: I think all men regret that they were not better men. And so do I. Specifically, I regret we could not have solved our sectional differences without war and the horrible bloodshed we have seen. I regret I have not been a better husband to Mary and a better father to my sons Robert Todd, Edward Baker, William Wallace, and Thomas, whom we call Tad. All of them are smart and loving and sometimes mischievous children. Sadly, we lost Eddie some ten years before we moved here to the White House. Then three years ago we lost Willie. Losing those two sons has been a heavy burden to bear. And, finally, I regret that I have not been a better friend to my friends. I resolve to do better by my family and my friends in the time I have left.

Grider: Sir, what are your plans for the future?

Lincoln: I've been a most unlucky president. Almost from the day of my inauguration, I've been burdened with a terrible war. Now I want to enjoy peace for the next three years of my term and help to repair the damages of war. I want to be able to relax and read and spend more time with my family and my friends. After I leave the White House, I might even want to write a book or two. I plan to move back to my home in Springfield. I want to visit Indiana and especially Kentucky and see my dear friend Speed. I'll practice a little law, but most of the time I just

Lincoln with his son, Tad.

want to be an ex-president and storyteller. Since I've been in Washington, I've got plenty to tell.

Now, it's about time for Tad and me to leave for Richmond. We're going down to reclaim Virginia and her sister states of the South and West and restore them to this grand old Union. Reconstruction will be a long and arduous task, but it can and will be done. I pray that God will direct our paths.

Grider: Thank you, Mr. President.

∼

A Lincoln Chronology

1809 — Born February 12, in Hardin County, Kentucky, now LaRue County, three miles south of Hodgenville, the son of Thomas and Nancy Hanks Lincoln.

1811 — In the spring the Lincoln family moves to a farm on Knob Creek, ten miles north of Hodgenville.

1812 — Another son, named Thomas, is born and dies in infancy.

1815 — In the fall Abraham and sister, Sarah, attend a nearby school for several weeks.

1816 — In December the Lincoln family moves to Perry County (now Spencer County) in southern Indiana, seventeen miles north of the Ohio River.

1818 — Lincoln's mother, Nancy Hanks Lincoln, dies from milk sickness, October 5.

1819 — Thomas Lincoln marries Sarah Bush Johnston, a widow, in Elizabethtown, Kentucky, December 2.

1823 — Thomas Lincoln joins Pigeon Creek Baptist Church, which the family attends, June 7.

1828 — Lincoln's sister, Sarah, who is married to Aaron Grigsby, dies in childbirth, January 20; Lincoln and Allen Gentry take a flatboat loaded with cargo to New Orleans, exact dates uncertain.

1830 — Thomas Lincoln leaves with his and his wife's families for Illinois; Lincoln drives one of three wagons, March 1; they locate ten miles southwest of Decatur on the north bank of the Sangamon River, March 15.

1831 — Lincoln, cousin John Hanks, and stepbrother John D. Johnston leave home and arrive in Springfield, Illinois, where Denton Offutt hires them in March to build a flatboat at Sangamon Town; from April through July, Lincoln pilots the flatboat, loaded with Offutt's merchandise, down the Ohio and Mississippi rivers to New Orleans (where he saw the brutal reality of slavery at street auctions), then returns to New Salem, eighteen miles northwest of Springfield; on August 1, Lincoln votes for the first time in New Salem; in September Lincoln is a clerk in Offutt's new store in New Salem.

1832 — Lincoln becomes a candidate for the Illinois legislature on March 9, favors improved navigation on the Sangamon River, changes in the usury (moneylending) laws, and universal education; New Salem men form a volunteer company to fight in the Black Hawk War, with Lincoln as captain, April 21; Lincoln is defeated in his bid for a seat in the Illinois legislature, August 6.

1833 — Lincoln and William F. Berry become partners in a store in New Salem, January 15; President Andrew Jackson appoints Lincoln postmaster at New Salem, a position in which Lincoln serves from May 7, 1833, to May 30, 1836, when the office is closed.

1834 — Lincoln becomes deputy surveyor of Sangamon County, January 6, and does surveying for three years; Lincoln is elected as a Whig to his first public office, as representative from Sangamon County to the Illinois House of Representatives, August 4.

1835 — Ann Rutledge, alleged lady friend of Lincoln, dies at her family's farm near New Salem, August 25.

1836 — Lincoln is reelected to the Illinois legislature, August 1; Lincoln receives a license to practice law in the Illinois courts, September 9, with final approval on March 1, 1837.

1837 — Lincoln supports a bill to move the Illinois capital from Vandalia to Springfield, February 24; Lincoln makes his first attack on slavery when he protests an antiabolitionist resolution in the House, March 3; Lincoln moves to Springfield, becomes a junior law partner of John T. Stuart, and rooms with Joshua F. Speed, April 15.

1838 — Lincoln is elected to the Illinois House of Representatives for the third time, August 6; Lincoln, a Whig, is defeated for Speaker of the House by a Democrat, December 3.

1839 — Lincoln is elected to the Springfield town board, June 24; Lincoln begins the practice of law on the newly organized Eighth Judicial Circuit and continues until he is nominated for the presidency in 1860, September 23; Lincoln is named a presidential elector by the state Whig convention, October 8 (he is also selected in 1844, 1852, and 1856); the Illinois legislature meets in Springfield, the new state capital, for the first time, December 9.

1840 — Lincoln is elected for the fourth time to the Illinois legislature, August 3; from August through September, he campaigns in southern Illinois for the Whig Party. In March, Joshua Speed's father dies and Speed announces plans to return to Louisville.

1841 — Lincoln is courting Mary Todd but has an emotional breakdown in early January; Lincoln leaves the law firm of John T. Stuart and becomes the partner of Stephen T. Logan, April 14; Lincoln goes to Louisville, Kentucky, to spend three weeks with his close friend, Joshua F. Speed, August–September.

1842 — A duel between Lincoln and James Shields is avoided when friends intervene, September 22; Lincoln and Mary Todd are married in Springfield in the home of the bride's sister, Mrs. Ninian W. Edwards, by an Episcopal priest, and they move into the local Globe Tavern, November 4.

1843 — The first of Lincoln's four sons, Robert Todd Lincoln, is born at the Globe Tavern, August 1.

1844 — The Lincolns buy and move into a home in downtown Springfield, May 1; Lincoln campaigns for Henry Clay in southern Illinois, Indiana, and Kentucky; he speaks at his boyhood home near Gentryville, Indiana, October–November; William H. Herndon is admitted to the bar and becomes the junior half of the Lincoln and Herndon law firm, December 9.

1846 — The Lincolns' second son, Edward Baker Lincoln, is born, March 10; Lincoln defeats his Democratic opponent, the Reverend Peter Cartwright, and becomes the only Whig congressman from Illinois, August 3.

1847 — The Lincolns spend most of November visiting Mrs. Lincoln's family in Lexington, Kentucky, then continue to Washington, where Lincoln takes his seat in the Thirtieth Congress, December 6.

1848 — Lincoln attends the Whig convention in Philadelphia and supports the successful candidate, General Zachary Taylor, for president; Lincoln speaks for Taylor throughout New England, September 12–22.

1849 — Lincoln supports a resolution in Congress to abolish slavery in the District of Columbia; he drafts an amendment to the resolution to provide compensated emancipation but never introduces it, January 10; Lincoln is admitted to practice before the U.S. Supreme Court, March 7; Lincoln declines the offer of the secretaryship of the Oregon Territory, August 21, and further declines the offer of the governorship of Oregon, September 27.

1850 — The Lincolns' second son, Edward Baker, dies after a protracted illness, February 1; Lincoln delivers a eulogy on the late President Zachary Taylor at Chicago's City Hall, July 25; William Wallace Lincoln, the Lincolns' third son, is born, December 21.

1851 — Abraham Lincoln's father, Thomas, born in Virginia in 1778, dies in Coles County, Illinois, January 17.

1852 — Lincoln eulogizes the late Henry Clay in Springfield, July 6.

1853 — Thomas "Tad" Lincoln, the Lincolns' fourth son, is born in Springfield, April 4; Lincoln allegedly uses watermelon juice to christen the new town of Lincoln, Illinois, named for him, August. 27.

1854 — Lincoln has lost much of his interest in politics over the previous five years, but he reenters the political arena following the passage of the Kansas-Nebraska Act, championed by Stephen Douglas, U.S. senator from Illinois, which will apparently open up the Western territories to popular vote to decide whether a new state will allow slavery, and thus repeal the Missouri Compromise, which has allowed Missouri into the Union as a slave state but prohibited slavery in future states that would be carved out of the territory of the Louisiana Purchase, May 30; Lincoln engages Douglas in a series of pivotal debates centered on the spread of slavery into the new territories; the two men meet for the first of their debates in Peoria, October 16; Lincoln is elected again to the Illinois legislature on November 7 but resigns on November 27 to campaign unsuccessfully for the seat of Senator Douglas.

1856 — In the spring the Lincolns have their home in Springfield enlarged from one and a half stories to two full stories; Lincoln is again a presidential elector and delivers a speech at the organization of the Republican Party in Illinois in Bloomington, May 29; the first Republican National Convention meets in Philadelphia, where

Lincoln receives 110 votes for vice president, June 19; Lincoln speaks in support of the Republican candidate for president, General John C. Fremont, at Kalamazoo, Michigan, August 27.

1857 — In the Illinois legislature meeting in Springfield, Lincoln attacks the *Dred Scott* decision of the U.S. Supreme Court, which held that temporary residence in a free state does not give a slave his freedom, June 26.

1858 — Lincoln is chosen by the Illinois State Republican Convention, meeting in the statehouse in Springfield, as candidate for the U.S. Senate, June 16; Lincoln and Stephen Douglas, the Democratic candidate, meet Aug. 21 for their first debate; from August through October, they meet at various Illinois locations for six more debates; beginning in Chicago on July 10, Lincoln makes at least sixty-three speeches during the campaign; in the election on November 2, Lincoln receives a majority of the votes, but because of the gerrymandered legislative districts, Douglas wins reelection to the U.S. Senate.

1859 — During 1859 Lincoln makes political speeches throughout Ohio, Wisconsin, and Kansas.

1860 — Lincoln delivers his highly acclaimed address at Cooper Union in New York City, February 27; Lincoln begins a two-week speaking tour of New England, February 28; The Illinois Republican Convention, meeting in Decatur on May 9 and 10, votes to support Lincoln for the Republican nomination for president; the Republican National Convention, meeting in Chicago, nominates Lincoln for president on the third ballot; the nomination for vice president goes to Hannibal Hamlin of Maine, May 18; after graduating from Phillips Exeter Academy in New Hampshire, Robert Todd Lincoln enrolls in July at Harvard University (upon graduation in 1864 he will become a captain on the staff of General Ulysses S. Grant); eleven-year-old Grace Bedell of Westfield, New York, writes to Lincoln on October 19 suggesting that he grow a beard—which he does; Lincoln defeats three other candidates—Stephen Douglas, Northern Democrat; John C. Breckinridge, Southern Democrat; and John Bell, Constitutional Union—and becomes the first Republican to be elected president of the United States, November 6; the secession of states begins with South Carolina, December 20.

1861— Lincoln pays a final visit to his elderly stepmother, Sarah Bush Johnston Lincoln, in Coles County, Illinois, January 31; the Confederate States of America is formed by delegates from South Carolina, Georgia, Florida, Alabama, Mississippi, and Louisiana; Kentucky-born Jefferson Davis is chosen to be president and Alexander H. Stephens of Georgia is chosen as vice president, February 4; Lincoln delivers his emotional farewell address to the people of Springfield from the rear of the train at the Great Western Railroad Station, February 11; after a twelve-day trip, punctuated by speeches and other public appearances, Lincoln arrives secretly in Washington, February 23; Lincoln is inaugurated as the sixteenth president of the United States, March 4.

Fort Sumter is attacked by Confederate forces and thirty-four hours later surrenders, April 12–14; Virginia, North Carolina, Tennessee, and Arkansas secede from the Union, April 15; President Lincoln blockades ports in South Carolina, Georgia, Alabama, Florida, Mississippi, Louisiana, and Texas, April 19; Lincoln suspends the writ of habeas corpus and blockades the ports of North Carolina and Virginia, April 27; Lincoln weeps publicly mourning the death of his young friend, Colonel E. E. Ellsworth, shot by a Confederate sympathizer after Ellsworth had removed a Confederate flag flying over a hotel in Alexandria, Virginia, May 24; Lincoln orders thirty days of mourning after the death of Stephen A. Douglas in Chicago at the age of forty-eight, June 3; Lincoln learns that the Union forces under General Irvin McDowell have been badly defeated at Bull Run, July 21; Lincoln places General George B. McClellan in command of all the troops in the Washington area, July 27; Lincoln issues an order forbidding commerce with states in insurrection against the government of the United States, August 16; following the resignation of General Winfield Scott, Lincoln designates General McClellan as the commander of the entire army, November 1.

1862 — The Lincolns lose their second son, William Wallace (Willie), February 20; the Union forces of General Grant and the Confederate forces of General Albert Sidney Johnston clash near a small church named Shiloh in Tennessee, with huge losses to both sides, April 6–7; General Robert E. Lee becomes commander of the Army of Northern Virginia, June 1; Lincoln admits publicly his policy on slavery in response to a critical editorial by Horace Greeley: "My paramount object in this struggle is to save the Union, and is not either to save or to destroy slavery," August 22; Lincoln issues his preliminary Emancipation Proclamation to take effect January 1, 1863, September 22; Lincoln replaces General McClellan as commander of the Army of the Potomac with General Ambrose E. Burnside, November 5; Lincoln approves the bill admitting West Virginia, which has seceded from Virginia, to the Union, December 31.

1863 — Lincoln issues the final Emancipation Proclamation, which frees slaves that are held in states that have seceded, January 1; General Robert E. Lee's invasion of Pennsylvania is ended by Union forces at Gettysburg,

Pennsylvania, July 1–3; Lincoln proclaims the first national observance of Thanksgiving, to be held on November 26, October 3; Lincoln delivers his address at the national cemetery at Gettysburg, November 19; Lincoln grants amnesty to Confederates who swear allegiance to the U.S. Constitution.

1864 — The National Union Party, in convention at Baltimore, nominates Lincoln for president and Andrew Johnson of Tennessee for vice president, June 8; Lincoln approves the act repealing the Fugitive Slave Act, June 28; Lincoln witnesses the Confederate attack on Fort Stevens on the outskirts of Washington, July 11; General William T. Sherman's Union forces occupy Atlanta, thus ensuring Lincoln's reelection, September 1; Lincoln is easily reelected, defeating the Democratic candidate, General George B. McClellan, November 8; Lincoln writes his letter of consolation to Mrs. Lydia Bixby, who has lost all five of her sons in the Union cause, November 21; Lincoln appoints James Speed of Louisville, brother of his friend Joshua F. Speed, attorney general, December 1; General Sherman captures Savannah, Georgia, and presents it to Lincoln as his "Christmas gift," December 22.

1865 — Lincoln approves the Thirteenth Amendment, which, when ratified by the states, will abolish slavery, February 1; Lincoln approves the act establishing the Freedmen's Bureau, which will assist the freed slaves,

March 3; Lincoln delivers his Second Inaugural Address, offering generous terms to the defeated Southern states as they reenter the Union, March 4; Jefferson Davis and his cabinet flee south from Richmond, Virginia, April 2; Union troops occupy Richmond, April 3; Lincoln visits Richmond, April 4–5; General Lee surrenders to General Grant at Appomattox Court House, Virginia, April 9; Lincoln delivers his final speech from a window in the White House, describing the condition of the Confederate states and a plan to bring them back into the Union, April 11; Lincoln is shot by actor John Wilkes Booth while attending a play at Ford's Theatre in Washington; April 14; Lincoln dies at 7:22 A.M. in the home of William Petersen, across the street from the theatre, April 15; funeral services are held for the slain president in the White House, April 19; the Lincoln funeral train leaves Washington on April 21 and takes a circuitous route west by way of Baltimore, York, Philadelphia, New York City, Albany, Buffalo Cleveland, Columbus, Indianapolis, and Chicago, arriving in Springfield, Illinois, at 9 A.M. on May 3; Lincoln is buried in Oak Ridge Cemetery in Springfield, May 4; it is later moved to the present memorial in Springfield.

1870 — Congress awards Mrs. Lincoln an annual pension of $3,000, which is later increased to $5,000, plus a one-time gift of $15,000.

1871 — Thomas (Tad) Lincoln dies of "dropsy of the chest" in Chicago, July 15, and his body is taken for burial to the Lincoln Tomb in Springfield.

1882 — Mrs. Mary Todd Lincoln dies in the Springfield home of her sister, Mrs. Ninian W. Edwards, the same house where she and Abraham Lincoln were married; she is buried in the Lincoln Tomb with her husband and three of her four sons.

1887 — Robert Todd Lincoln and his wife present the Lincoln home in Springfield to the State of Illinois, June 16.

1926 — Robert Todd Lincoln dies and is buried in Arlington National Cemetery, July 26; he has earlier deposited his father's papers in the Library of Congress.

Sources of Illustrations

Unless otherwise indicated, all images are from the Library of Congress (LOC).

Page 6, Kimmel & Forster lithograph of a Henry Thomas painting.

Page 10, photo by Alexander Gardner; 1863.

Page 15, attributed to Nicholas H. Shepherd, 1846.

Page 19, statue by Leonard Crunelle.

Page 29, 1896 poster, Wade Hall Collection.

Page 32, undated drawing by unknown artist, Wade Hall Collection.

Page 37, Lester Jones for the Historic American Buildings Survey, 1940 (LOC).

Page 44, unnamed photographer, Detroit Publishing Co. (LOC).

Page 49, 1887 drawing from *Century* magazine, based on a photograph of Herndon; Wade Hall Collection.

Page 53, attributed to Nicholas H. Shepherd, 1846.

Page 55, Currier & Ives lithograph, published 1867.

Page 61, photo by Alexander Hesler, 1860, Springfield, Illinois.

Page 67, photo by Alexander Gardner, March 4, 1865.

Page 68, letter from A. Lincoln to Lydia Bixby, 1864.

Page 71, photo of Lincoln and son Tad, 1864, by Anthony Berger of the Matthew Brady Studio.

About the Author

Wade Hall holds degrees from Troy University, the University of Alabama, and the University of Illinois. He has taught at all three universities, as well as at the University of Florida, Kentucky Southern College, and Bellarmine University, where he chaired the English, humanities, and arts programs. He is the author of numerous articles and reviews and more than twenty books about Kentucky, Alabama, and the South. In 2005 he published *The Kentucky Anthology: Two Hundred Years of Writing in the Bluegrass State*. He served in the U.S. Army in the mid-fifties in several states and in Germany. He now lives in his boyhood home near Union Springs, Alabama.